The Spirit of
VICTORY

A Sports Devotional

Jeremy Dover, Travis Barnes,
Peter Nelson

The Spirit of Victory
Copyright 2021 © Star Label Publishing

Published by Star Label Publishing
P.O. Box 1511, Buderim, QLD, Australia
Email: publishing@starlabel.com.au
Interior design: Rebecca Moore
Cover art design: Tony Moore

1st Edition July 2021
All rights reserved. No part of this publication may be reproduced in any form; stored in a retrieval system; or transmitted; or used in any other form; or by any other means without prior written permission of the publisher (except for brief quotes for the purpose of review or promotion).

Scripture quotations marked (NIV) are taken from the Holy Bible, New International Version®, NIV®. Copyright © 1973, 1978, 1984, 2011 by Biblica, Inc.™ Used by permission of Zondervan. All rights reserved worldwide. www.zondervan.com. The "NIV" and "New International Version" are trademarks registered in the United States Patent and Trademark Office by Biblica, Inc.™

Unless otherwise noted, all Scripture quotations are from The Holy Bible, English Standard Version® (ESV®), copyright © 2001 by Crossway, a publishing ministry of Good News Publishers. Used by permission. All rights reserved.

Scripture taken from the New King James Version®. Copyright © 1982 by Thomas Nelson. Used by permission. All rights reserved.

Scripture quotations from the Authorized (King James) Version. Tights in the Authorized Version in the United Kingdom are vested in the Crown. Reproduced by permission of the Crown's patentee, Cambridge University Press.

Scripture quotations marked CSB have been taken from the Christian Standard Bible®, Copyright © 2017 by Holman Bible Publishers. Used by permission. Christian Standard Bible® and CSB® are federally registered trademarks of Holman Bible Publishers.

Scripture quotations marked (CEV) are from the Contemporary English Version Copyright © 1991, 1992, 1995 by American Bible Society, Used by Permission.

The views expressed here-in remain the sole responsibility of the author, who exempts the publisher from all liability. the author and publisher do not assume responsibility for any loss, damage, or disruption caused by the contents, errors or omissions, whether such contents, errors or omissions result from opinion, negligence, accident, or any other cause, and hereby disclaim any and all liability to any party.

ISBN: 978-0-6484602-9-9

This book is dedicated to the glory of God.
He gave us the great gift of sport
so we might know Him and
enjoy Him forever.

Table of Contents

Foreword by Rev. Dr Mark Tronson............................7

The Goal of this Book..11

1. The Greatest Victory...19

2. Drowning In Honey..25

3. Keep Walking..29

4. Wrestling with God..35

5. Ambassadors of Encouragement....................41

6. The Upside of Down Days.................................45

7. Picking a Captain..51

8. Changing Teams...57

9. Playing with Joy...63

10. The Great Exchange..67

11. Prayer Coach...73

12. Winners In Life...79

13. Fight the Good Fight!...83

14. Coach's Voice..89

Notes..95

Foreword

by Rev. Dr. Mark Tronson

The Olympic Games has provided Christian athletes and coaches, along with Christian sports missions, an open door to speak into the hearts of fellow athletes and those who enjoy the sports. This has been a big part of my ministry.

My Olympic story is twofold, one of Olympic ministry and one an Olympic field hockey writer and five books on hockey. In 1984 I was the industrial chaplain for two days a week at Shell Australia in Sydney—the Australian Olympic champion and IOC Vice President Kevan Gosper AC was also the Chairman of Shell Australia. Concurrently, I was the Australian cricket team chaplain. The two came together and I was invited to be a Chaplain at the LA Olympics in 1984 and wrote hockey for The Australian newspaper.

It was a privilege to appoint Australian chaplains to the Seoul, Barcelona and Atlanta Olympics 1988, 1992,

1996 and Sydney 2000. In February 2000, Kevan Gosper invited me to travel to the IOC in Lausanne Switzerland to develop with IOC staff the Religious Services 'Transfer of Knowledge'—sent to the following host city.

In 2009 my wife Delma and I travelled to the Winter Olympic host city Vancouver, Canada where we met with Olympic officials on the Religious Services program planned for the 2010 Winter Olympics. Then, at a glittering dinner in Dallas Texas hosted by the Olympic Chaplaincy ministry led by Sam and Sharon Mings (LWFC)—Olympian of the Century, Carl Lewis presented Delma and I the 'Olympic Ministry Medal'.

Meanwhile from 1992 I opened for the Australian Institute of Sport an elite athlete respite lodge 'Basil Sellers House' in Moruya—for the following 14 years we hosted the various sports units and many Olympian visits where I gave a short Bible passage reflection.

Atlanta and Sydney Olympic chaplain and the Australian Institute of Sport chaplain for 30 years, the Reverend Peter Nelson, wrote for Christian Today:

"I've worked very closely with Mark Tronson and have a great respect for what he has done in establishing chaplaincy across the board in all sports since 1982, and his Australian Cricket chaplaincy from 1984 and

founding the Basil Sellers athlete respite facility in Moruya in 1992—these achievements are recognised from the highest official to the newest athlete.

Timeout in Moruya was perhaps the single most important factor in making effective my ministry as the AIS chaplain. Athletes over many years visited Moruya and were ministered to by Mark and Delma Tronson. Mark gave them a Bible talk and handed sports New Testaments to each young athlete. Many a time when doing room inspections these Bibles were found beside their beds. It has been my privilege on many occasions at their initiative to speak with these young athletes when returning from Moruya.

When Mark was away there were times I went to Moruya and gave the Bible talk to the athletes. I arranged for various international visiting athletes to visit Moruya. This Moruya excursion became a highlight for all elite athletes in their stay at the AIS, I cannot emphasise this enough. Meeting Mark's great support, Mr Basil Sellers AM, on his visit to the AIS was very important for as Mark reminded me again today, that the Scriptures exclaim, the Lord sent Basil Sellers for 'such a time as this'."

I have been a witness to the way sport and the Olympics can be used to share God's love and grace with others. I have seen the Olympics embrace faith into their psyche.

I have seen respite ministry used as a tool to point to the Prince of Peace. I have seen God raise up servants, such as Basil Sellers, to drive this ministry. And I know this devotional book will continue this legacy for Christ. I highly commend this Olympic book.

Rev. Dr. Mark A. Tronson

Our overall goals:
Aiming for gold

"Not to us, Lord, not to us, but to your name be the glory, because of your love and faithfulness."
Psalm 115:1

This book aims to bring honour and praise to God. In all we do, Jesus gets the glory, not the athletes. We want you to read our sporting devotionals and say, "Praise be to the God that saves through Jesus!" ***not*** "Wow, those athletes are so amazing."

This book brings together three authors who love Jesus, who have studied and written about the Bible over many years, who have served in ministry, including within sport. It was written as a sporting devotional for each day of the Tokyo Olympics, however, it has application for anyone wanting to grow in their knowledge of God.

Bible

The primary way God reveals Himself is through the Bible. The Bible is 'God breathed' and we want to be faithful to the Biblical text. It is this text that has the power to work hand-in-glove with the Spirit to change lives. Our job, as authors, is to point to this Gospel of grace from these Bible passages. Our aim is to allow God's Word to speak by unpacking the passages and challenging you in its application for your life.

As a result, our devotional will have a focus of bringing you, the reader, into God's Word using sport and the Olympics as the vehicle to point you to Jesus. It is this Gospel, revealed in the Bible, which transforms. I like Tim Keller's quote explaining this:

> *"Let the Gospel sink so deeply down in you that it changes your views and even the structures of your motivation."* [1]

All of Life

"For the sake of My Holy Name" Ezekiel 36:22

All parts of life, including sport, are for God's glory. There is no dualism of a secular and sacred. Jesus is Lord over Saturday sport, as He is Sunday church. The Apostle Paul talked about sport and the Isthmian Games in a way that reflected this theology that all of life is for God's Holy Name. I want you to finish this book knowing that God is interested in sport and the Olympics because, as my Theology Professor summarized well, *"Wherever people are, God is interested!"* [2]

Sport & the trinity
Let me get a little technical and "nerd-out" for a moment. There is an incredible depth to faith and sport. Sport has a unique and complex place in our world. For example, the Olympics carries historical, cultural and social factors meshed within a political and national identity. The Games themselves try to bring peace, a Pax Romana, to the world. However, this legacy is questionable, as Sport Sociologist Paavo Seppänen explains,

"The modern Olympic Games have grown into a social and cultural spectacle without parallel in kind or scope. In spite of its goals of mutual understanding, the Olympic movement has been quite powerless in promoting peace and understanding. Rather, it has become an institution whose primary function is the consolidation of the existing order. Not the individual athlete but the nation-state is the primary unit of the Olympic system. Olympics are misused for political purposes. They depend on the world power balance and on business and are best described by the trinity of Nationalism, Commercialism and Athletism." [3]

While this hegemonic trinity fails to transform human hearts, sport does provide the perfect universal language for the Gospel to permeate. The true Triune God uses sport many times in the Bible to move from the physical reality we know to spiritual realities we must see.

The Bible is asking us to transpose[4] the temporary struggles and training we see in sport to a spiritual level. For example, when we watch Olympic boxing, we are to see beyond the physical to a different kind of fight: the spiritual. When we witness a gold medal victory we are to look beyond the physical to a deeper eternal victory.

Our focus should be to transpose the lessons from the Bible into every area of life. Dutch pastor and politician, Abraham Kuyper's famous quote, summarizes the Gospel's reach:

> *"There is not a square inch in the whole domain of our human existence over which Christ, who is Sovereign over all, does not cry, Mine!"* [5]

The Gospel: Setting the rules of the game

Many people already have a preconceived idea of the Gospel[6]. However, to ensure we are all at the same starting line, here is a Gospel summary. Read it, understand it but more importantly, wrestle with how it calls you to respond.

The Four P's of the Gospel of grace

God's Position – God is our loving Creator. He made us for a reason: to have an active relationship with Him. He gave us sport to enjoy life and worship Him. God's position is He wants us to glorify Him and enjoy Him forever.

Our Problem – Our problem is that we reject His love. We break this relationship with Him and as a result our relationships with others are broken. We reject God and as a result God should reject us. In sport we call it getting a Red Card for breaking the rules and a Sin Bin awaits.

While we use sporting metaphors to understand our problem, separation from our loving Creator is serious for both us and God. The core of the issue is our broken relationship with God. In one of the most moving verses in the whole Bible, the impact of this broken relationship is seen in Genesis chapter 6 verse 6 explaining that our sin grieves God to His heart.

God's Provision – While we were still rebels, God sent Jesus to take our Red Card and restore us to full Life. The good news is that Jesus reconciles us to God by taking the penalty of sin for us and giving us His perfect record. And the amazing thing is that this is given as a gift: undeserved, unmerited, amazing grace.

Our Possibility – We have a choice. This Gospel of grace becomes an invitation offered to all. Our possibility is to receive this free gift of Life. Jesus used a term "Shalom" or peace to describe the possibility we have. We have the possibility of no longer being rebels fighting against God and deserving the sin bin. Now, because of Jesus, we can have a deep peace with God that transcends all understanding. This provides direction for life. It gives focus for our sport and provides Life in all its fullness.

The one thing sport _cannot_ teach us
Sport reflects many of these key Gospel components of sin bins, sacrifice, and victory. However, the one thing sport **cannot** fully understand is *grace*. A God so amazing that He would search after us and reveal His love to us through Jesus as an underserved *free gift*. Sport operates on performance: earning a reward. The Gospel operates on an underserved *free gift:* grace. This is the God we will discover in this sporting devotional.

Game plan
The three authors of this book have different styles of explaining the Bible passages, however they all dig deep into the text. Reading the Bible and doing a Bible based

devotional involves several steps to unearth the treasure of the Gospel. This is the format we will use in our devotional:

- **Title** - provides a summary and overview of the passage.

- **Coaching Tips** - provides the context of the passage. It gives coaching tips on how God used the historical context to speak to the original audience. Understanding the context, key words and writing style offer coaching tips leading to a deeper understanding of God's Word and a Spirit-driven application for us today.

- **Going for Gold** - provides the meaning of the passage. It is the unpacking of the passage's key themes in context of the Gospel.

- **Training** - provides application, from the text, to achieve the goal of the passage.

The Greatest Victory

By Jeremy Dover
1 Corinthians 15: 54-58

At the end of this training session you will have a deeper understanding of Jesus' mission through the Old Testament, to the church in Corinth and to us today.

Coaching tips:
In approaching this passage, you need to have a good set of Nike shoes to run through the context of the Old Testament.

Gospel
The author (the Apostle Paul) has been outlining the greatest victory of all time. He has been describing the historical and theological facts of Jesus' death and resurrection. He starts (1 Corinthians 15:3) by outlining the heart of the Gospel: The "Christ" (meaning God's

Anointed One) died for our sins, He was buried, was raised from the dead and appeared before many, as historic fact. And all this was prophesied as the central message of the Old Testament (a.k.a. "according to the Scriptures"). It is vital to note that the Old Testament contains the same Gospel message of salvation as the New Testament. There is only one way for salvation and it all points to Jesus. In fact, it is one continuous story of God reaching out to a fallen people and restoring them through Jesus.

Nike

Nike is one of the biggest sporting companies in the world today, however the name comes from the ancient Greek god of victory. Their logo, the "swoosh," comes from the sound and way a runner breaks through a finishing tape.

The ancient Greeks believed their nike god would fly to the battle to pronounce "victory" for one side. Today, we watch the world's greatest athletes doing battle, each seeking victory over their opponents. Nike is mentioned here in the original Greek text of 1 Corinthians chapter 15. Paul talks about Jesus winning nike ("victory") over sin and death. With this context, let's look deeper into the Bible to learn more about Jesus.

Going for Gold:

The same battle analogy can be seen when an athlete

wins gold. They stand victorious over their opposition. In ancient times the victors received a floral wreath as a prize, however this flora would die. Today, our winners receive a gold medal which will outlast the athlete's own life, however, it will still tarnish over time. In contrast, Jesus' victory impacts past, present and future.

Jesus' substitutionary death and resurrection from the dead saves all who lived *before the cross*. For example, Adam and Eve had hope that God would send the One to undo that first death and crush the serpents head. Jesus also saves all *today* who look back to the cross and trust in Jesus to restore that broken relationship. And it will save all *to come* in the future who call on the name of Jesus. The victory of the cross is THE pivotal moment in history.

In this passage Paul proclaims the good news that the battle has been won! Like a prized Olympic boxer, Paul trash-talks death; "Where, O death, is your victory? Where, O death, is your sting?" Now that Jesus has paid its price in full (Isaiah 25:8; Hosea 13:14) Paul gives death a persona to mock its impotence.

The Gospel
The equation Paul explains is simple:

1. It was sin that brought us under death's power.

Sin is often misunderstood but it is described as an active rebellion against God's loving will. The word actually has a sporting origin. It comes from the sport of archery. An athlete takes aim at the target but misses the mark: The athlete's arrow falls short. In the same way, sin is defined as falling short of God's perfect standard (Romans 3:21).

2. The penalty of sin is death. Death is described in the Bible as both physical death as well as a spiritual death i.e., a separation from the loving God.

3. However, Paul explains that, thanks to Jesus, we are gifted Jesus' own victory. His victory means we, as part of His team, share in this victory. That is momentous news, if you have not grasped it yet!

Training:

How can we apply this victory today? Have a look at the swoosh on any Nike top you own. What side is it on? It is always over the left chest. This is just the general branding strategy. Now compare this with the swoosh on an Olympic athlete's clothing. Which side is it on? Athletes representing their countries requested their national symbol to be over their heart (left side). It is a symbolic gesture that the most important thing over their heart is their country.

Lay our medals down

It is the same for a Christian. All our gold medals, all of our own victories and all of our achievements need to be removed from our heart and replaced with Jesus. Our own achievements pale into insignificance when compared with Jesus' victory. Ironically, our achievements only find their true richness and significance when seen in the shadow of Jesus' victory.

Like the Nike swoosh, Christians do not see "just a cross" but this object symbolises the fact that Jesus has conquered death and we live in the shadow of that great victory. Lay your own victories down and place Jesus' victory over your heart.

Waiting for the victory that has already come

Jesus' first coming and victory means His second coming makes more sense. When He returns, He comes as the victorious Lord of all. His first victory will be completed or consummated in His second coming. This should cause us to continue to train hard. Prayer for others, learning more about Him (a.k.a. reading the Bible, Bible studies, engaging with sermons etc.), caring for those in need, and seeking justice are all lived out in Jesus' victory. This victory gives us focus as we actively wait for His return.

Prayer:

Dear Lord, I give you thanks for the victory you have won for me over sin and death. I lay my own victories down and place Jesus' victory over my heart. Forgive me when I struggle with pride and help me to wait patiently and actively for Jesus' return.

Drowning In Honey

By Peter Nelson

"It is not good to eat much honey. Nor is it glorious to seek one's own glory."
Proverbs 25:27 (ESV)

In some unfortunate circumstances, bees can drown in their own honey. But the saying "drowning in honey" is one that I learnt on the cricket field. A batsman is scoring run after run from his favourite shot. It is his day and he knows it as runs flow from his bat. But, overuse of his favourite shot (some would say overindulgence) results in his dismissal. As the bowler and fieldsmen celebrate, the word is passed around "he drowned in honey". Honey is sweet and enticing, but too much can be sickly. Seeking one's own glory and promoting one's self can be sweet and enticing, but it is a false and passing glory. It is another way of drowning in honey.

Success in any area of life is sweet but it can be much harder to handle than failure. Fame from success can produce big heads but small hearts. Doting on success can soften us and lead to forgetting all who have sacrificed and guided us along the way.

Two questions arise:
1. What can we glory in?
2. Whose glory can we seek?

Firstly, Jeremiah the prophet spells it out magnificently in Jeremiah 9:23-24 (NKJV),

> Thus says the Lord: "Let not the wise man glory in his wisdom,
> Let not the mighty man glory in his might,
> Nor let the rich man glory in his riches;
> But let him who glories glory in this,
> That he understands and knows Me,
> That I am the Lord exercising loving kindness, judgement and righteousness in the earth.
> For in these I delight," says the Lord.

The focus is not on self and its achievements but upon God and His greatness. To know and love and thank Him frees us from the small world of self-obsession and self-image and opens our eyes to see real and lasting glory.

Secondary, whose glory can we seek? In 1 Corinthians

10:31 Paul passes on his own motivation for living:

> Therefore, whether you eat or drink, or whatever you do, do all to the glory of God. (NKJV)

Here is living at its best, doing all to the glory of God. This all-encompassing—do **all**, from the simple acts of eating and drinking to competing at the Olympic Games or leading a nation or caring for a family. Whatever we do let it be for the glory of God, so He can be obeyed, honoured, thanked, and praised by all.

Prayer:
Lord of all glory and wisdom, we find it so easy to focus on self, we are all part of the selfie-generation. Turn our eyes to see your great purposes for the universe and for our lives. Give us the strength, wisdom, and motivating love to do all things for your glory. In the name of Jesus. Amen.

3.

Keep walking

Travis Barnes

"But those who hope in the LORD will renew their strength. They will soar on wings like eagles; they will run and not grow weary, they will walk and not be faint."
Isaiah 40:31 (NIV)

At the end of this training session, you will be challenged to continue to follow Jesus even on dark and difficult days.

Coaching tips:

The book of Isaiah is one of the longest books in the Bible with 66 chapters. The Prophet Isaiah ministered to the people of Judah during the reigns of kings Uzziah, Jotham, Ahaz, and Hezekiah. God gave Isaiah messages for the people of Judah and its capital Jerusalem. Isaiah's messages were hard to hear; Isaiah predicted God would send judgement upon Judah for their idolatry and corruption.

God's people were once slaves in the nation of Egypt where they were cruelly mistreated. God's people cried out to Him to save them from the cruelty of the Egyptians. God heard their prayers and sent Moses to lead His people to freedom. God led His people into a land of their own.

God's people were told they would remain in the land while they remained faithful to him. God wanted His people to be a light to the surrounding nations, displaying God's goodness and justice to all. Sadly, God's people rarely obeyed him; they quickly abandoned God to worship idols. God's people were often selfish, violent, and unjust. God sent many prophets to warn and correct His people so they would turn back to Him. However, they would often close their ears to the prophets, laugh at their warnings, and harshly persecute them. Isaiah declared that God would use the violent nation of Babylon to bring Jerusalem crashing down for its rebellion. God's people would be evicted from their land and go into exile in Babylon.

The book of Isaiah isn't solely about God's judgement of Jerusalem. It is also about hope for God's people that He would one day restore His people to their land: that God would renew His relationship with His people. Isaiah chapter 40 begins this theme of hope that despite their sin God had not abandoned His people; there was hope for a new future. God's people would once again put their hope in the Lord and soar on wings like eagles.

Going for Gold:
When I studied teaching at University, I quickly made friends with Jared who lived locally and was a very fit runner. One day after class Jared asked me if I wanted to go for a jog. We ran for about eight kilometres at a frantic pace. At the end of the eight-kilometre circuit, I was completely exhausted. I had spent every ounce of energy just trying to keep up. I was lying on the ground, puffing and panting and Jared said to me, "Want to go for another lap?" I went home, Jared ran the course again and I guess that's why he became an Olympic Gold Medallist.

In 2008 at the Beijing Olympics Jared Tallent burst onto the sporting scene. He won a bronze medal in the 20-kilometre walk and a silver medal in the 50-kilometre walk. In 2012 Jared completed the 50-kilometre walk in 3 hours and 36 minutes winning another silver medal. It was difficult for Tallent to accept the result; he had long suspected the winner of being a drug cheat. It took four long years but eventually, Tallent was vindicated. The winner was disqualified and Tallent was upgraded to the gold medal and Olympic record holder. It was a long walk to gold. There must have been days that Tallent thought he would never receive his gold medal; that justice would never come. Just like a walking race, Jared continued step after step with great patience and determination.

The nation of Israel had been crushed by the Babylonian exile. Some must have wondered if their exile would ever end, if God would ever restore His people. Isaiah 40 is a chapter of comfort for God's people weary and wounded by exile. The chapter finishes by encouraging God's people to put their hope in the Lord and in their weakness look to God for strength.

Training:
If you're going through a challenging time right now; don't give up and don't despair. Jared Tallent eventually got his gold medal and God's people were delivered from exile in God's timing. God will not leave you in this difficult season forever; it's a season that will eventually pass.

Don't rely on your own strength and your own wisdom to get yourself through a difficult time, rather turn your eyes to God's strength and seek His wisdom. God can use difficult times in our lives to teach us things that we might not learn any other way. Use this time to wait upon Him, to rest in His goodness, to remember His faithfulness, and to trust that He will work all things together for the good of those who love Him. Keep walking towards that Hope.

Prayer:
God on this difficult day, I choose to trust in your goodness and your faithfulness. Help me to continue living for you day by day and moment by moment. I look forward to your deliverance and trust that you will work all circumstances together for good. Amen.

4.

Wrestling with God

Jeremy Dover
Genesis 32

Coaching tips:

In approaching this passage, you need to know that wrestling with God is good, wrestling with the world is pointless and that Jesus didn't tap.

The context of this passage is important. Jacob, like us, was a person searching for belonging. He searched for acceptance from his father, Isaac (whose dad was Abraham). He searched for it from his potential father-in-law, Laban (Genesis 29). He searched for it from his potential bride, Rachel. However, God used this never satisfying pursuit for blessings to lead him to a wrestle that would change his life.

Going for Gold:
In wrestling, the aim is to try and bring your opponent to a position of submission. You search for a point of weakness in which they "tap out." That is, they tap the mat as a signal they have submitted to the pain and acknowledge the superior strategy of their opponent. At this point, the bout is lost.

In Genesis chapter 32, Jacob wrestles with God. He had been wrestling with others all his life—from wrestling with his brother, Esau in the womb, to his father-in-law Laban.

Jacob was a man searching for acceptance and meaning in life. Each pointless wrestling project moved to the next, never satisfying. Now he was all alone in the dark wrestling with a man of equal strength, yet so powerful that He could dismember Jacob at a touch of his hip.

In wrestling, controlling the head or hip are the critical points to gain submission over an opponent. Jacob's opponent (God Himself) disables his hip by a touch and then transforms his mind. With light approaching, Jacob realises that he is actually wrestling with the Divine. The one thing he had been searching for his whole life, acceptance from God, was now right in front of him. So important was it, that he was willing to face death than let it go (remember, God is holy, and no one can see the face of God and live; Exodus 24:10; 33:23; Numbers 12:8; Isaiah 1). The result is God blesses Jacob, he is given a new name that his family adopt (Israel), and he finds a true meaning in life in the promises of God.

Training:
Jacob and his nation's story reflect our own story: wrestling with life to find meaning. Athletes often search for meaning in the skills they develop, the safety of their familiar sporting routines and the fame or acceptance they find in these sporting communities. However, none of these satisfy on a deeper level. From God's acceptance flow blessings that transcend all understanding.

So, what do you do when you finally find something so great you would rather die than let it go? That was Jacob's wrestling story. And it is our story too. True blessing and acceptance in life come from Jesus. And searching after Jesus is our take-home training tip.

This journey Jacob faced, and we all face, points to Jesus who IS that blessing. The three great promises made to Abraham (Genesis 12) and witnessed by Jacob are fulfilled in Jesus as the true blessing to the nations. Jesus wrestled with the greatest enemy, sin and death, to reconcile us to God: the Just for the unjust, the Righteous for the unrighteous, so that we can have peace with God.

However, in this wrestling, Jesus didn't tap. Jesus did not submit to temptation or evade this self-sacrifice. He conquered sin and death and won the victory through His resurrection. How thankful we should be!

Life after gold
Winning Olympic gold does not fully satisfy. This was shown in research I conducted as part of a University and Australian Government funded research team. We interviewed 18 Australian Olympic Gold medal winners and their coaches[7]. Our aim was to examine the impact winning gold had on their lives.

Their experiences as gold medallists mirror Jacob's search for meaning. These Olympic champion's pursuit of this goal had many positive aspects. For example, personal satisfaction in achieving a major goal. However, a majority (17 out of the 18) reported a significant number of negative experiences associated with their win. For example, tall-poppy syndrome and extra pressures and expectations. One athlete shared that the silver medallist had congratulated him after his win but also reminded him that he was only champion for one day; the next competition would be a different story!

Winning gold is an amazing achievement! However, as Jacob found, real meaning in life comes from a deeper understanding of how God's plan transforms your life's plan.

Searching for God means wrestling with His plan. It means seeing Jesus' victorious wrestle with sin on our behalf. And it means acknowledging the Holy Spirit's power in turning our lives from 'finding acceptance in others' to 'finding acceptance in God'.

Paul explains (Ephesians 6:12 KJV):

> For we wrestle not against flesh and blood, but against principalities, against powers, against the rulers of the darkness of this world, against spiritual wickedness in high places.

Prayer:
Thank you, Heavenly Father for your plan to save us. Thank you, Lord Jesus as the One who didn't tap but died so we might live. Thank you, Holy Spirit for helping us towards true Life in its fullness. We praise you Father, Son and Holy Spirit.

Bonus: If you want to read more about God's plan and Jesus not tapping, can I recommend two books? These will bless you immensely in seeing how your life fits into God's plan as well as the critical way you should have the cross as the centre of your faith. Vaughn Roberts, *God's Big Picture* and Donald MacLeod, *Christ Crucified*.

5.

Ambassadors of Encouragement

Peter Nelson

"No foul language should come from your mouth, but only what is good for building up someone in need, so that it gives grace to those who hear it."
Ephesians 4:29 (CSB)

If anyone tells you "sticks and stones can break my bones, but names will never hurt me," don't believe them! Words are like bullets that can puncture the thickest skin and pierce the hidden soul. Sportsmen and sportswomen are constantly targeted by vile trolling and anonymous criticism and judgement. Our voices, which we think are so important, are but the microphones of the heart. If words can bring such hurt, they can also bring great good. So why not use our words to bring encouragement, praise and thankfulness?

In a recent book entitled *Encouragement - Adrenalin for the Soul*, the author, Mark Chanski challenged the readers to become 'Ambassadors of Encouragement'. Think of the different atmosphere encouragement would bring to the family circle, to the workplace and to our institutions! Genuine encouragement would lift our sportsmen and sportswomen to face adversity and overwhelming challenges with a renewed confidence.

The verse from the letter to the Ephesians (chapter 4 verse 29 CSB) eliminates the negative and accentuates the positive in our speech. 'No foul language should come from your mouth, but only what is good for building up someone in need.' A few verses earlier, Paul wrote in verse 25, 'Put away lying, speak the truth, each one to his neighbour.' Through our words of encouragement, we can add value to the life of our neighbour who has been made in the image of God.

Above all, these words bring grace to the hearers. Grace is one of the GREAT words of the Bible and has its origins in the concept of gift and generosity. It is a word that wonderfully reveals what God is like in His character and activity. As Psalm 116:5 puts it, 'The Lord is gracious and righteous, our God is compassionate.'

God, as the author of life, is the giver of all good things. However, God's grace goes way beyond the second mile, when in sheer generosity God gives eternal life to undeserving sinners through the death and resurrection of Jesus Christ. It is goodness and generosity beyond imagination. Grace also conveys the idea of extra strength being communicated to the hearer.

In our speech, we faintly reflect the grace of God when we encourage and build up others, in another letter Paul wrote, 'Let your speech always be gracious, seasoned with salt, so that you may know how you ought to answer each person' Colossians 4:6 (ESV).

When we add to encouragement, praise and thankfulness to the menu of our speech, we have something tasty and appetising for every hearer. The wise words of Proverbs 15:4 (NKJV) sum it up, 'A wholesome tongue is a tree of life.' The world needs ambassadors of encouragement, including the sporting world, so commit yourself today to becoming one.

Prayer:
Gracious Lord,
Please let my words be wholesome, uplifting and encouraging. Give me an attitude within to always want to communicate grace, hope and joy. Amen.

6.

The Upside of Down Days

Travis Barnes

"Consider it pure joy, my brothers and sisters, whenever you face trials of many kinds, because you know that the testing of your faith produces perseverance. Let perseverance finish its work so that you may be mature and complete, not lacking anything."
James 1:2-4 (NIV)

At the end of this training session, you will be challenged to embrace the trials and tests that come your way because they help you to grow in perseverance.

Coaching tips:

The letter of James was written by none other than the half-brother of Jesus: a later son of Mary and Joseph. During Jesus' ministry, James was not a follower and did not believe He was God's appointed Saviour. His family believed that Jesus was out of His mind. After Jesus rose from the dead, He appeared to James which was enough to convince him that Jesus truly was God's own son. After the resurrection, James became a significant leader in the Church in Jerusalem. In James' letter, he doesn't boast about his family connection to Jesus, he simply refers to himself as a slave of Christ.

James had firsthand knowledge of the tests and trials that Jesus faced. Being mocked and ridiculed, through to his own bloody death on a cross. He writes this letter not to a specific Church but to God's people scattered all over the world. In this letter, he will challenge you to put your beliefs into real-life practical action.

Going for Gold:

Kim Brennan was a young athlete with plenty of potential and a dream to compete in the Olympic Games. Leading up to the 2004 Olympics she was the second-fastest hurdler over 400 meters in Australia. Tragically, Brennan's Olympic campaign was derailed by injury. She developed a stress fracture in her foot. She went through rehabilitation trying to get herself right in order to compete, but the injury kept reoccurring until it became obvious that she couldn't run anymore. Kim Brennan's athletic career was over at just 19 years of age. She was forced to watch the 2004 Olympics on television.

Because Brennan couldn't run, she kept fit by using a rowing machine. A rowing coach thought her technique was solid. Eventually, she was persuaded to try out rowing on the water.

After just three years of rowing, Brennan went to the 2008 Olympic games. She returned to the Olympics in 2012 winning a bronze and a silver medal. In 2016 she won a gold medal at the Rio Olympics and carried the flag for Australia at the closing ceremony. Kim Brennan would have been devastated when her injuries ended her hurdling career, but I wonder if she's grateful that her adversity guided her towards rowing.

In this passage, James is encouraging believers to see the upside of down days. He says that a trial is an opportunity for pure joy. Most people are happy when their trials are over; James wants believers to be joyful when they begin! Instead of throwing a pity party when times are tough, James wants you to throw an actual party and rejoice because your trials are going to achieve something good.

In the Old Testament, there's a story about a boy called

Joseph who has great dreams of becoming a leader. No sooner does he have these dreams than his brothers betray him and sell him into slavery. As a slave Joseph is falsely accused and thrown into prison—so much for those dreams. In the prison, Joseph assists one of the Kings' servants and years later that servant recommends that the King summon Joseph for his help. Joseph is eventually made a great leader in Egypt and prepares the way for God to save His people from slavery all via many trials. And through these trials we see the nation of Israel established and the Saviour of the nations, Jesus, come. I'm sure Joseph became a stronger, more courageous, humbler leader because of the years of trials he faced before arriving at the palace.

Brennan, Joseph, and James were all stronger for the trials they faced. God can use your tests and trials too.

Time for training

James says trials produce perseverance; difficult times force you to rely on God's strength instead of your own. Trials tend to make people less self-reliant and more God-reliant. As God helps you face each trial; remember His faithfulness. Next time you face a difficult test you'll remember that God was faithful to you in the last challenge. This will give you confidence as you face challenges in the future. The more challenges you face the more you'll learn to trust God and rely on His strength. After years of facing all kinds of tests and trials with God's help, you'll be a stronger, more resilient, humbler, more mature follower of Christ. You won't fall apart at the first sign of trouble, instead, you'll calmly look to God and encourage others to do the same. The way to grow your perseverance is to trust God in the challenge you're facing today and ask God to show you the upside of this down day.

Prayer:
God help me to see the positives in this negative situation. Help me to trust you and rely on Your strength; not mine. God, in the days ahead may I come to see your faithfulness in this situation and may it build my trust in you for the future. Amen.

7.

Picking a Captain: Which team are you on?

Jeremy Dover
Romans 5:12-21

Coaching tips:

Paul is writing to the church of Rome outlining the problem *all* humanity faces: sin and death. However, he also contrasts this with the solution found in Jesus. This section of Paul's letter is a powerful Spirit-filled lesson in God's overall plan to reconcile His people to Himself. And he uses a powerful pattern imbedded throughout the Bible: A leader represents God's people and that leader's success, or failure, is credited to the whole team.

The best example of this 'Federal Headship' is David and Goliath. Firstly, a disclaimer: that passage is ***not*** about being brave like David. Bravery is important however that is not why it is included in the Bible. David and Goliaths' battle is about two representatives acting on behalf of their nation. If one wins, *that* nation wins. This forms the coaching tips for unpacking Romans chapter 5.

In the past our representative was Adam. He was 'sin-binned' and as a result, everyone on his team fell under his penalty. Contrasting this, Jesus comes as 'the second Adam,' and through His perfect life, death and victorious resurrection He wins a great victory for everyone on His team.

This leadership concept is beautifully highlighted by the literary style that moves from 'the one man,' Adam, to Jesus contrasted by His righteousness, obedience and grace. God's Word is amazing in that not only the words but even grammar is God breathed!

Relationship Restoration

The whole Bible, I believe, can be summarized in two words: '*Relationship Restoration.*' Adam and Eve's rebellious actions against God red-carded the whole human team. Yet, Jesus' obedient actions, including His actions on the cross, mean that all who acknowledge Him as their Captain receive His victory. This had been prophesied right from the start. God explained the plan that He would send someone (a.k.a. the Messiah/Christ/

Anointed One) to crush the serpent's head. That is, destroy sin and death and restore the relationship.

Going for Gold:

Imagine a spotlight that switches to highlight two sporting captains on the field. As one's actions are highlighted the spotlight shines on him. Then it moves to the contrast of the other's actions. The spotlight moves back and forward between the two captains, each time contrasting the differences between them. This is a distinctive literacy style used by Paul to contrast Adam to Jesus. The 'protasis' and 'apodosis' switch the spotlight between death and life, trespass and gift, judgement and grace, condemnation earned, and righteousness gifted, disobedience bringing death and obedience imputing life. As the spotlight switches between captain Adam and Captain Jesus the contrast is made about how bright Jesus is in comparison. Jesus is described with His 'Christ' title as God's Anointed One to fix Adam's problem.

Training:

Picking captains—The first training challenge comes from Jesus described here as *OUR* Lord. It is a personal invitation to make Him my Lord. To choose Him as the Captain means we receive His victory. It is the same in sport when a captain accepts the champion's trophy on behalf of their team. The supporters cry out, "WE won!" even though they never set foot on the field. The application is we have to pick a captain, so pick Jesus!

Victory—Jesus is described in the Bible as the 'first fruits'. This means that because He died and was the first to rise again, all that are on His team will follow the Captain: when we die, because Jesus has conquered sin and death, we also will rise again. The good news is that death has been beaten. This un-natural condition, that appeared after the Fall (Genesis 3), has been destroyed by Jesus' atonement and victory displayed in His resurrection. The application is to give thanks and celebrate this victory you share in.

Grace—Wednesday afternoon school sport found us on the basketball court. It was a diverse group with strong sporty types such as Andrew and Jimmy and those that were still to develop some coordination such as best mates, Chris and Diego. Our teacher chose Andrew and Chris to be 'captains' and pick, one-at-a-time, their teams. It was a lesson I never forgot. This selection process was normally a horrible practice because the best athletes were chosen first until the less sporting types were embarrassed at the end.

Andrew started with the obvious pick, Jimmy. He was tall and a natural basketballer. Then it was Chris's pick. He did not even scan the class for who was the next most athletic but immediately called out his bestie, "Diego".

He had chosen his friend over athletic prowess. He had made Diego the first pick rather than leave him on the pile till last. I remember that afternoon because it was so counter-cultural. Relationships triumphed over utilitarianism.

While our Romans chapter 5 passage reminds us we must pick a captain to represent us, Romans also reminds us that God has chosen us, *by grace*. We are not chosen because we can help the team win Olympic gold but simply because of our relationship with Jesus. Romans 5:20-21 explains this saying that grace reigns all the more. The application is to never forget our restored relationship is a gracious gift. Yes, we must make a choice to pick Captain Jesus, however this happens as a result of God graciously picking us.

Prayer:
Gracious Lord, I want to be on your team. I want to have Jesus' victory credited to me. I understand this is only possible because you give it as a free gracious loving gift. Thank you.

8.

Changing Teams

Travis Barnes
Colossians 3

At the end of this training session, you will be challenged to embrace your identity as a citizen of heaven and no longer play by the old rules of earth.

Coaching tips:
Things couldn't be more different for Paul, the author of the letter to the Colossians. He previously opposed the followers of Jesus and everything they stood for. He would hunt them down and harshly persecute Christ's followers to the point of death. When he encountered Jesus for himself everything changed. Instead of opposing Jesus, he started proclaiming Jesus. Instead of being the persecutor of other Christians, he became persecuted for being one. His friends became his enemies, and his enemies became his friends. Even his name was changed

from Saul to Paul.

This letter to the Colossians was written from jail; a place that Paul had become very familiar with since following Jesus. Paul wanted Christians to know that when we turn to Christ things change. We have a new identity as children of God and new citizenship in God's kingdom. Paul once wrote that when we turn to Jesus, we become a new creation; the old is gone and the new has come.

If you were to move countries, you would discover your new country would have different rules and customs. They might drive on the other side of the road, use a different currency, and have traditions that you've never heard about before. You would be wise to pay careful attention to the customs and laws in your new country to avoid embarrassment or trouble.

Paul is telling his readers that they have left their old lives behind, and we now live with a new identity in a new kingdom.

Going for Gold:
Jana Pittman was the best hurdler in the world. In 2003 and again in 2007 she won the 400-meter hurdles world championships. Unfortunately for Pittman things never came together for her at the Olympics. At a warmup event for the 2004 Olympics, Pittman tore cartilage in

her right knee. Pittman underwent surgery just a week before the Olympics and remarkably battled her way into the Olympic final. She finished 5th in the final; injuries prevented her from making the Olympics in 2008 and 2012. Pittman retired from athletics but in a turn of events, she took up the sport of bobsledding and competed at the 2014 winter games. In doing so Jana Pittman became the first female Australian athlete to compete at the summer and winter Olympics. There are significant differences between hurdles and bobsled; as Pittman trained, she became a faster sprinter and more muscular in order to have the explosive power needed for a bobsled race.

Jana Pittman changed from one sport to another. Paul says we've gone through an even bigger change; we've moved kingdoms! In the first chapter of Colossians, Paul says that we've been rescued from the kingdom of darkness and transferred to the kingdom of God's Son. Our old lives were characterised by greed, lust, anger, bitterness, lies, and pride. These things are very common in the kingdom of this world, but they have no place in God's kingdom. Paul says we are to take off our old nature and put on our new nature. This is like getting changed to go to a party; off come the tracksuit pants and our grubby t-shirt and we put on new clothes. Citizens of God's kingdom are characterised by tender-hearted mercy, kindness, humility, gentleness, and patience.

Paul goes further and says in this new kingdom it doesn't matter if you are a Jew or a Gentile, slave or free, circumcised or not. Those things don't matter anymore. Imagine being a dentist in Kenya but on arrival in Australia you are told that Australia doesn't recognise your qualifications. Your qualifications mattered a lot in one place but don't matter at all in another. In our world, people value those who are rich, famous, attractive, smart, and seen to be successful. Those things don't matter in God's kingdom; the labels and titles of our old life don't count anymore. You're a child of God and a citizen of heaven and that won't change whether you have a Ph.D. or a criminal record.

Training:

Like Jana Pittman, we've changed teams and we need to learn a whole new way of living. How much time do you invest trying to be accepted by the standards of this world? How much energy do you spend trying to be judged successful by a kingdom you're no longer part of? The dollars in your account, your followers on Instagram, and your awards all pale into insignificance compared to your identity as a citizen of God's kingdom. That's the most important thing on your resume. Paul wrote that we shouldn't conform to the customs and patterns of this world. Paul said that instead, we should let God transform our thinking so that we think about the things of heaven not the things of earth.

Prayer:

God thank you that you have transferred us from the kingdom of darkness to the kingdom of your Son. Help me to learn how to live as a citizen of your kingdom. May I leave behind the customs and the thinking of my old life and embrace my new identity as a child of God and a citizen of heaven. Amen.

9.

Playing with Joy

Peter Nelson

"Do not sorrow, for the joy of the Lord is your strength."
Nehemiah 8:10 (NKJV)

After winning the women's 20/20 World Cricket Cup the headline in the newspaper stood out so boldly "JOY IS THE AUSTRALIAN'S SECRET WEAPON."[8] The player of the match, Alyssa Kealy, said that the joy of essentially playing for fun was something she valued. She added, "you cannot wipe the smile off my face." Later she commented, "That freedom and pure enjoyment in what you're doing is lost a bit in men's professional sport."

Alyssa really strikes at the essence of sport as a bringer of joy. Sportspeople can bring joy to the spectators who love to appreciate their skills, their artistry and the pure commitment of each player. Think of a Federer v Nadal tennis match. In order to bring joy, the players themselves must play with joy, zest and enthusiasm. In the 1970's Jacques Ellul, a French sociologist expressed a fear that sport was becoming too mechanical and an expression of work, not play.

The balancing of the work and play aspects of their profession is a constant challenge to professional sportspeople. If all the theories about the reasons for sport could be laid end to end, they would cover the rail track from Sydney to Perth. But sport as a bringer of joy resonates deeply with me. I am thankful for all the sportspeople who have brought that joy into my life.

In life, we can bring joy to others, but only if we possess it ourselves. In Nehemiah's time about 430BC the city of Jerusalem's walls needed rebuilding and the hearts of the people needed to be uplifted. The city had been destroyed by enemies and people had been subdued by captivity in that far off place, Babylon. Through hard work and co-operation, the city's walls were rebuilt and, through the reading of God's word by Ezra, the hearts of the people were deeply moved and uplifted. Nehemiah wanted the people to see that their God was a God of joy, even for exhausted people. In Deuteronomy 28:47 God condemns those in Israel who did not serve the Lord their God with joy and gladness of heart. Heaven is a place of joy where there is even more joy when one sinner on earth repents (Luke 16:7).

Jesus said to His disciples in the Upper Room the night before His crucifixion "These things I have spoken to you, that my joy may remain in you and that your joy may be full" John 15:11 (NKJV). Peter, one of those disciples there on that night, wrote later, "...whom having not seen you love. Though now you do not see Him, yet believing, you rejoice with joy inexpressible and full of glory" (1 Peter 1:8 NKJV). After love, joy is listed second in the list of the fruit of the Spirit. Paul encourages the Philippians to "Rejoice in the Lord always" (Philippians 4:4).

Are we bringers of joy? Whether in the sporting arena, or at work or in the home or among our friends and colleagues.

Prayer:
Thank you, Lord, for the many things we can be joyful about. You have blessed us with our physical needs, with family and friends, and with the joy of sport. We thank you for the greatest blessing: Jesus. Help us, by your Spirit to be people that reflect this joy to all around us, for your glory.

10.

The Great Exchange

Travis Barnes

"God made him who had no sin to be sin for us so that in him we might become the righteousness of God."
2 Corinthians 5:21 (NIV)

At the end of this training session, you will be challenged to marvel and be amazed by the great exchange that Jesus initiated on the cross.

Coaching tips:
Isaiah chapter 53 sums up our problem: We all like sheep have gone astray, each of us has turned to our own way. God made a wonderful world for us to live in. It was a world without brokenness, a world of love, joy, peace, and unity. People were in right relationship with God and right relationship with each other. The first humans

and every human since has chosen to ignore God's wisdom for living and gone their own way. Humanity's sin separated us from God and threw us into a world of brokenness. Humanity found itself in a world of suffering and selfishness far from God and at odds with each other.

Isaiah 53 also describes a suffering servant who will take humanity's sin upon himself. He is described as a man of suffering, familiar with pain who was pierced for our transgressions and crushed for our iniquities. Jesus was innocent and we were guilty but in the biggest plot twist in history, Jesus traded places with us. Jesus received the punishment for our sin and disobedience, and we received His forgiveness and mercy. Charles Spurgeon said you stand before God as if you were Christ because Christ stood before God as if He were you.

Jesus hung on a cross and was held responsible for every sin from lying to murder and everything in between. Every cruel word, every lustful thought, and every act of revenge was placed on him.

Paul writes in his second letter to the Corinthians that Christ had no sin but took our place and became sin for us so that we might become the righteousness of God.

This is the great exchange; Christ received everything wrong about you so that you could receive everything that's right about him.

Going for Gold:
In March 2004 Australia's swimmers were competing at the Australian championships for a spot on the Olympic team. In the men's 400 metres freestyle Ian Thorpe was a heavy favourite. He was the world record holder and won the gold medal at the previous Olympics. As Thorpe lined up on the blocks for the start of the race the unthinkable happened; he overbalanced and fell in the pool. Thorpe was instantly disqualified. He couldn't qualify for the event despite being the fastest swimmer in the world. Grant Hackett qualified first, and the relatively unknown Craig Stevens qualified in second place.

The Australian media could see a gold medal slipping away and campaigned strongly for Thorpe to be reinstated for the Olympics. The problem was that two Australians had already qualified for the event; there wasn't room for three. The only way Thorpe could be selected for the men's 400 metres freestyle would be for Hackett or Stevens to step aside and let Thorpe swim. After several weeks of deliberation, Craig Stevens gave up his spot in the race. It was a big sacrifice to make; the Olympic games don't come around every day. Ian Thorpe went to the 2004 Athens games and won the gold medal in the 400 metres freestyle.

Ian Thorpe and Craig Stevens swapped places. Stevens made the sacrifice; Thorpe received all the benefits. This is what happened when Christ died in your place on the cross. Christ made the sacrifice so you could receive the blessing of being restored into right relationship with God.

Imagine going to a swap meet where people buy and sell second-hand goods. You'll find a table with old computers, cassette tapes, and CD-ROMs. Somebody else is selling old car parts, another table has old garden tools and there's a table dedicated to selling homemade jams and spreads. Imagine that Jesus is at the swap meet and he's going to swap with you. He's going to take all your wrongdoing, all your guilt, He's going to take all your sin and selfishness and replace it with all of His righteousness and all of His purity. This is the great exchange! He's going to take everything that's wrong with you and replace it with everything that's right about him.

Training:

I could turn up at your house on Christmas day and offer you a present. It might be a wonderful present that cost me a lot of money. If you don't let me in when I knock on the door, if you don't accept the gift I'm offering then all my effort, all my sacrifice was for nothing. Jesus hung on a cross so you could receive His forgiveness and be in right relationship with God. Have you received His forgiveness? Have you opened the door to Christ? Have you turned to Christ and asked Him to be the king of your life?

Prayer:
Jesus, thank you for the great exchange. Thanks that you took our sin and we received your forgiveness. Thanks that you did for us what we could never do for ourselves. I ask for your forgiveness, I ask that you would be king of my life this day and every day. Amen.

11.

Prayer Coach

Travis Barnes
Psalm 51

At the end of this training session, you will be challenged to admit your failings to God and allow Him to create a clean heart within you.

Coaching tips:
King David wrote this Psalm at one of the lowest moments of his life. When David was a boy, he was visited by the prophet Samuel who anointed him to be the next King of Israel. When he was still a boy, he defeated the giant warrior Goliath. David won so many battles people began singing, "Saul has killed his thousands and David his tens of thousands" (1 Samuel 18:7). King Saul became jealous of David and sought to have him killed. David spent years on the run until Saul's death.

Then David finally became the King of Israel. David was loyal to God during those difficult years on the run. It was when he was in the comfort and security of the palace he began to succumb to temptation. One evening David was walking on his roof when he spotted a woman bathing. David noticed the woman was beautiful and enquired about her. David was told her name was Bathsheba, the wife of Uriah the Hittite. Uriah was not a stranger to David; he was one of David's best and most loyal warriors. Uriah wasn't at home because he was at war fighting on behalf of the king. David knew him and David betrayed him. He sent for Bathsheba and slept with her.

Things become complicated when Bathsheba discovers she's pregnant. Bathsheba's pregnancy was difficult to explain given Uriah's absence. David tried to cover up his sins by asking Uriah to come home. He hoped Uriah would sleep with his wife and assume the baby was his. Uriah returned from war, but such was his loyalty he thought it would be improper to go home and sleep with his wife. In solidarity with Israel's troops, he sleeps at the entrance to the palace. David was desperate to cover his sin and attempted to get Uriah drunk but even this plan failed.

Having failed to cover up his sin, David committed another. David sent Uriah back to the battle; he gave Uriah a note to hand to his commander. The note instructed his commander to ensure Uriah was killed in battle. Once Uriah's death was arranged David took

Bathsheba to be his wife. Israel was unaware of David's corruption, but God knew. God sent the Prophet Nathan to confront David.

When confronted, David confessed his sin and in the process of his repentance he wrote Psalm 51 asking God to create a clean heart within him.

Going for Gold:
In 2004 Tyler Hamilton won a gold medal for the United States in the men's individual time trial. Hamilton was a big name in cycling and competed in the Tour De France. Winning Olympic gold was the high point in Hamilton's career but months later it would be followed by his lowest moment when he tested positive for blood doping. Hamilton had been a drug cheat since 1997. He justified his actions based on his belief that almost everyone in cycling was also cheating. Hamilton was banned for two years but denied any wrongdoing. Upon his return to cycling Hamilton continued to cheat. In 2009 Hamilton tested positive for drugs and was banned for eight years. The suspension ended his cycling career. In 2010 he confessed that he had taken performance enhancing drugs throughout his career. Hamilton said that when he confessed to cheating, a weight came off his shoulders.

In Psalm 51 David comes clean and asks God to cleanse him of his guilt. David is done with cover-ups and pretending. David has hit rock bottom and asks God for mercy.

Training:
It takes a lot of energy to keep up appearances. It's stressful telling lies hoping you won't be found out. You might be able to fool people for a short while, but God knows the truth. Are you tired of playing games and pretending? Then it's time to come clean with God and ask for his forgiveness. Jesus has already taken the punishment for your sin when he died in your place. Now is the time to ask for the forgiveness that Jesus purchased on the cross.

In Psalm 51 David acknowledges his sin, that it wasn't just sin against Uriah or Bathsheba but against God. David asks God not to banish him from His presence but to restore the joy of His salvation; that David would once again willingly obey the Lord. You too might wish to pray the words of Psalm 51 asking God to restore the joy of your salvation to you once again. Towards the end of the Psalm, David says that God doesn't desire sacrifices but rather He desires a broken and contrite spirit. God doesn't want you to attempt to earn His favour through great deeds of sacrifice but rather through a humble and repentant heart.

Prayer:
God, I confess my sin to you and seek your mercy. Create in me a clean heart and renew a loyal spirit within me. May I once again experience the joy of your salvation. Amen.

12.

Winners In Life

—

you can be a loser in sport, but still be a winner in life

Peter Nelson
Psalm 1

Psalm 1 sets the pace for the rest of the Psalms with its first word *'Blessed.'*

Psalm 150 ends the Psalms with *'Praise'* mentioned in *every* verse.

In the Psalms every human emotion from exultant joy to deep sorrow to anger is expressed. John Calvin wrote that Psalms reveal "an anatomy of all parts of the human soul." Furthermore, in its poetry, words take on a sharper meaning, and poetry has a way of expressing feelings that prose cannot.

Psalm 1 focuses on the godly life versus the ungodly life. The advice given to the godly is carefully arranged in a progression:

- Not *walking* in the counsel of the ungodly
- Not *standing* in the way of sinners
- Not *sitting* in the seat of the scornful

From the negative, the Psalmist moves to the positives of:

- Delighting in the Law of the Lord
- Meditating day and night upon God's Law

Such a person has a life of fruitfulness, usefulness and is a blessing to others. He or she is just like a tree planted by a river. Fruit comes at the right time and the leaf does not wither. Here, we are given a picture of life and wholeness and human flourishing.

One of the great men I have had the privilege of meeting in life was Ron Williams. Ron was an Aboriginal elder and evangelist who travelled all over Australia, bringing the good news of Jesus to all. Ron was the father of Lydia, accomplished goalkeeper for the Matilda's (the

Australian Women's Football team). When Lydia was playing junior football, the team lost many games. After such losses, Ron would go and encourage the entire team with the same words, "Remember girls, you can be a loser in sport, but still be a winner in life!" What wisdom is distilled in those words!

Winners in Life
Psalm chapter 1 is about being a winner in life, despite all the things that would hinder us and come against us. The key to winning lies within. It is delighting in the Law of the Lord so that it is not only read but joyfully obeyed. This is the way Jesus lived every day and even though He died upon a Cross, friendless and forsaken, He rose again from the dead, prospering forever and being able to give new life and hope to all who approach Him.

Jesus is under no illusion of what will make us winners in life. In John 16:33 He says to the disciples "These things I have spoken to you, that in Me you may have peace. In the world you will have tribulation; but be of good cheer, I have overcome the world." (NKJV)

To be a winner we must overcome adversity, opposition and hostility. Romans 12:21 says, 'Do not be overcome by evil, but overcome evil with good.' Paul, along with other believers, faced trials, distress, persecution, famine and many other dangers. However, he could still say, "yet in all these things we are more than conquerors through Him who loved us" (Romans 8:37). To be a winner in life we need the love of God within us, the Holy Spirit to strengthen us and God's Word to guide us.

Prayer:
Almighty and loving God,
Give me a genuine love for You and Your Word. Give me a heart to obey and enjoy living every day for you. By Your strength alone make me an overcomer. For the sake of the Lord Jesus, the great overcomer in life and death. Amen.

13.

Fight the Good Fight!

Following Jesus all the way to the end

Travis Barnes

"I have fought the good fight, I have finished the race, I have kept the faith."
2 Timothy 4:7 9 (NKJV)

At the end of this training session, you will be challenged to stick with Jesus right to the end.

Coaching tips:
The book of 2nd Timothy is one of Paul's last letters.

Earlier in Paul's life, he was a committed opponent of Jesus. He was determined to arrest and have His followers put to death. In those days he was known as Saul of Tarsus and Christians everywhere were terrified of him. Saul travelled to Damascus on a mission to arrest and kill more Christians when he was interrupted by Jesus himself. The encounter was so powerful Saul was totally changed. He stopped arresting Christians and became one himself!

From that time Saul was known as Paul and he boldly declared that Jesus was King. Instead of putting Christians into jail, people were now putting him into jail. He wasn't guilty of anything other than proclaiming Jesus, but the Roman authorities kept him under lock and key.

One time Paul listed the trials he went through because he proclaimed Jesus. These included beatings, stonings, prison time, whippings, shipwrecks, and constant danger from Jews and Gentiles. God gave Paul the strength to endure these trials, the strength to love and forgive his enemies, and the strength to proclaim Jesus right to the end. Paul once said, "Christ gives me the strength to face anything" (Philippians 4:13 CEV). Paul was writing to Timothy who he had mentored in the faith and was a Christian leader at the Church in Ephesus. Paul tells Timothy that his death was not far away.

He wanted Timothy to know that he had fought the good fight, he had finished the race, he had remained faithful. This is something all Christ-followers should hope to be able to say in our final days.

Going for Gold:
Shaunae Miller-Uibo is a track and field athlete from the Bahamas. In 2016 she was in the final of the 400 meters sprint. She was up against American Allyson Felix, a six-time Olympic gold medallist. Shaunae-Miller started strongly and was leading, heading towards the finish line when Allyson Felix pulled up alongside her. The race was neck and neck with Allyson Felix looking stronger and Shaunae-Miller beginning to struggle. In the final metres of the race, the unthinkable happened. Shaunae-Miller dived for the line. It's unclear whether her diving was deliberate or whether she simply collapsed having given her all. In a photo finish, it was Shaunae-Miller's dive that made the difference giving her the gold medal in one of the most memorable Olympic finals in history. Shaunea-Miller ran a personal best time of 49.44 with no one in any doubt that she gave it everything.

Shaunae-Miller left nothing in the tank in her pursuit of gold and Paul too had given his all in the pursuit of a much bigger prize. Paul stuck with Jesus through some incredibly difficult circumstances. What was the secret to his endurance?

I believe the secret to his endurance was that he treasured his relationship with Jesus and never lost sight of eternity.

Paul wrote about his past life and his many credentials[9]. Paul said he once thought these things were important but now, he considered them worthless compared to the infinite value of knowing Jesus. Paul treasured Jesus so much that he was willing to withstand all kinds of punishment. Both Roman and Jewish authorities locked Paul up and took away his freedom, but they could never take away his greatest treasure: Jesus.

Paul never lost sight of eternity. He knew that his real home was in heaven and so didn't get distracted from his God-given mission. Paul knew that while he was still alive, he could do fruitful work for Christ and his imminent death would bring Paul home to be with Jesus.

In an Olympic final an athlete might keep playing even though they are injured. They might be in obvious pain and yet they play on. The reason is simple: they want to win the prize! The athlete's pain will be temporary, but the gold medal will be theirs forever. That's how Paul kept focused on his mission and endured suffering; he treasured Jesus and never lost sight of the prize!

Training:
Is Jesus your greatest treasure? Is He more than a story?

Is Jesus more than something you believe and something you attend? Is He someone you follow and a cause that you live for? To fight the good fight and follow Jesus all the way to the end, He must be your greatest treasure.

The tests and trials of life, the good and bad things that happen will test whether Jesus is truly the king in your life.

Prayer:
Jesus, I want you to be my greatest treasure. May I treasure knowing you and seek to know you more deeply every day. May I not lose sight of eternity; may I remember that my earthly life is short. May I fight the good fight of faith all the way to the end. Amen.

14.

Coach's Voice

Peter Nelson

*"Therefore everyone who hears these words of
mine and puts them into practice
is like a wise man who
built his house on the rock.
The rain came down, the streams rose,
and the winds blew and
beat against that house;
yet it did not fall, because it had
its foundation on the rock.
But everyone who hears these words
of mine and does not put them
into practice is like a foolish man
who built his house on sand.
The rain came down, the streams rose,
and the winds blew and beat against that
house, and it fell with a great crash."
Matthew 7:24-27 (NIV)*

Being a coach is a tough gig. Your destiny is tied up with your teams' performances. As a result, coaches pour themselves into their work and give of themselves unstintingly to their players and their club.

A coach must be a multi-skilled operative. He/she is an expert in their chosen sport, on top of all the technical details, an instructor, a tactician, a motivator, a psychologist, a counsellor, a manager of people, a confessor, an authoritarian, a friend, a CEO yet servant to the club and players. Who would want to be a coach? If the team succeeds it is all credit to the players. If the team loses it is the fault of the coach.

In Australia, a coach (unlike many authority figures) is held in the highest regard and with utmost respect. Legendary coaches in Australian sport like Jack Gibson, Wayne Bennett, Joyce Brown, Kevin Sheedy, Jock McHale, Laurie Lawrence, Harry Hopman, Bob Simpson are household names. When coaches speak, players listen!

Perhaps one of the best ways to describe Jesus' ministry on earth is that of a coach. He had a small team of 12, plus a larger following. He instructed them in the ways of the Kingdom of God and was preparing them to be His messengers to the world.

In the sporting environment, there is no place to hide, and any weakness of a coach is quickly spotted by the players. Questions are raised. Can they do or have done what they teach? Can they handle pressure? How do they deal with setbacks? Do they have a presence about them?

Two great aspects of Jesus as coach are that He practised 100% of what He taught and handled pressure magnificently. His Sermon on the Mount (recorded in Matthew chapters 5-7) didn't take long to deliver but His listeners knew that the Speaker lived every word of that sermon every day. Nobody walked the walk or talked the talk as thoroughly as Jesus. But all coaches want to see their players to be quick to listen and ready to put into practice what has been communicated.

The Sermon on the Mount is like an inspiring vision statement delivered by a coach at the beginning of the season. It outlines the kind of person the coach requires for his team as well as a code of conduct for anyone who wants to be part of the successful team. After an inspiring presentation by a coach, players clap enthusiastically, feel super-motivated and have a clear direction for the season ahead.

At the end of Jesus' message, the listeners were amazed at His authority. But as you read it you might well say 'What a great message! What a great teacher!' and feel the need to applaud. But wait a minute! As you read the sermon you will note that it ends on judgement and that it requires total obedience from the heart. In life, on our way to eternal life we need more than a coach, even the very best one. We need a Saviour. Someone who can take away our sins and who can give us a righteousness that pleases God and who can provide us with the inner motivation and power to obey the Coach's words.

Jesus is not only the great Coach in life, but also the magnificent Saviour. He died to take away our sins and His own (100%) righteousness is credited to those who trust Him. On top of that, Jesus gives to believers His Holy Spirit to fulfil a mind-blowing Old Testament prophecy from Ezekiel 36:26-27:

> I will give you a new heart and put a new spirit within you: I will remove your heart of stone and give you a heart of flesh. I will place my Spirit within you and cause you to follow my statutes and carefully observe my ordinances. (CSB)

Prayer:
Everlasting Lord,
As I read Your message from the mount, I recognise Your greatness as a teacher and coach. But the message reveals my own shortcomings and sin. I look to You to be my Saviour and to give me that new heart. Amen

Notes

[1.] P.12 — Twitter @timkellernyc Jan 13, 2017

[2.] P.13 — Dr. David Wilson https://thebarnabasconnectiononline.wordpress.com/about/

[3.] P.13 —Seppänen, P. (1984). "The Olympics: A Sociological Perspective." *International Review for the Sociology of Sport*. 19(2):113-127.

[4.] P.13 —C.S. Lewis calls it "transposition" — taking God's created realities, and the culture we create, and seeing through them to the ultimate reality.

[5.] P.14 —Abraham Kuyper: A Centennial Reader, ed. James D. Bratt (Eerdmans, 1998), 488

[6.] P.14 —Greek word meaning *"Good News"*

[7.] P. 38 —Life after Winning Gold: I. Experiences of Australian Olympic Gold Medallists in The Sport Psychologist, Susan A. Jackson 1 , Jeremy Dover 1 and Lisa Mayocchi 1
1 The University of Queensland
DOI: https://doi.org/10.1123/tsp.12.2.119

[8.] P.63 —Lalor, P. T20 World Cup: Joy is the Australian's Secret Weapon. The Weekend Australian (9/1/21)

[9.] P.86 —See Philippians chapter 3:4-10

www.ingramcontent.com/pod-product-compliance
Lightning Source LLC
Chambersburg PA
CBHW050320010526
44107CB00055B/2328